WHEN'S LATER, DADDY?

Bil Keane

FAWCETT GOLD MEDAL • NEW YORK

WHEN'S LATER, DADDY?

Published by Fawcett Gold Medal Books, a unit of CBS
Publications, the Consumer Publishing Division of CBS Inc.
by arrangement with The Register & Tribune Syndicate, Inc.

ISBN: 0-449-14124-1

Printed in the United States of America.

18   17   16   15   14   13

"Oh, boy! Can WE play, too, Mommy?"

"I didn't do it. I can scribble better'n that."

"The letter X stands for a kiss, X marks the spot
or a movie we can't see."

"You put the penny in and I'll flush it."

"Sam guesses EVERY TIME which hand I have
the dog biscuit in!"

"Telephone, Billy! It's a girl."

"I can wink, see?"

"Of COURSE Grandma likes little boys. But, this time she's invited DOLLY to stay with her for a few days."

"Bye, Mommy! I'll phone when I get there ---
if I'm not too busy helping Grandma!"

"I get to sleep in Dolly's room!"
"No! I do, Mommy! Me!"
"I said it first!"

"Gee, Grandma! I didn't know you liked to play with all these things."

"I better not lock the bathroom door, Grandma,
'cause I might lock myself in and you'd have
to climb through the window to get me out."

"Yes, I'm rememberin' my manners...yes, I'm helping Grandma...yes, I'm eatin' all my vegetables...come on, Billy get off the phone and let me talk to Mommy!"

"It's a good thing Billy and Jeffy aren't here
'cause they'd eat up all the cookies. Can I
have some more, Grandma?"

"Why do we have to take another nap, Grandma?
I'm not tired."

"Hi, Mommy! This is Dolly. Grandma and I just had breakfast. Last night we watched Johnny Carson."

"If Grandpa went to heaven just before I was borned maybe he picked me out for Mommy and Daddy."

"When I grow up, Grandma, I might come and live with you all the time."

"That's not the kind of peanut butter Mommy buys. That's not our kind of bread. This is a different milk. . ."

"Grandma! That lady called you Florence! I
never knew you had a REAL name!"

"...and Mommy gets mad at Daddy when he's late gettin' home, and Daddy doesn't know where the money's comin' from to pay all those bills, and PJ wets the bed, and Billy kicked the school principal, and..."

"Don't worry, Grandma, I'll just tell Mommy that we got sick and tired of that pony tail."

"Wait! I'll leave my doll here with you,
Grandma, so you won't be too lonely
after I'm gone."

"Gracious me! You're all a sight for sore eyes.
Land's sake, Jeffy, how you've grown while
I've been at Grandma's! Doesn't my hair
look SPIFFY? Goodness! I'm famished
for a cup of tea. . . "

"I liked it better bein' an only child at Grandma's."

"Why does the driver sit on one side of the bus
when she picks Billy up and on the OTHER
side when she brings him home?"

"I would have gotten a hundred if I hadn't missed those six problems."

"Last one in is a
rotten egg!"

"Mommy, Billy called
you a rotten egg!"

"I don't like this kind of bread. It has FRECKLES on it."

"Daddy, lift me up so I can make a basket."

"Hurry up and open it so I can see what
I got you."

"Bite down hard on it with your hind teeth."

"Can't I leave this hair long right here? It's the only way I can grow sideburns."

"Close your eyes and ears. I want to tell
Mommy a secret."

"Mommy said to tell you I had a very nice time."

"I didn't want the skin off my apple. Can you put it back on for me?"

"Here's a picture of Mommy when she was building PJ."

"I like that perfume you wear in the morning, Mommy — toast and bacon."

"Move over, Daddy — I can't see."

"Mommy! You said you'd save me the juice cans so I can make you a pencil holder at school!"

"Pretend you're calling Mommy and Daddy on the phone -- that'll make them behave."

"You don't 'spect me to play that do you? It's for ages three to six — I'm SEVEN!"

"While you're up there, Daddy, see if you can
find my rocket and frisbee, and Jeff's glider
and Dolly's yellow ball and..."

"I don't care. That's why I put on lots of perfume -- to keep the boys AWAY from me."

"Now P.J. can reach a hand to hold, too!"

"But, I've got my own money to buy it!"

"It's Sam blowing the horn. I guess he wants
us to hurry."

"Do you think God would mind if I killed this fly?"

"That's for me! I'll get it!"

"Aw, what a gyp! I just PRETENDED I was
takin' a nap and I fell asleep for REAL!"

"Here's a nice bone for Sam if he's being a good dog and not up on the furniture."

"What ELSE did you see at the zoo
besides flies?"

"And whose little boy are you?"

"Nonebody's."

"Billy's eating the cookies out of his lunch and
the bus hasn't even come yet!"

"But, Daddy! How does all that snow get
UP there?"

"Mommy! Will you be mad if we tell
you somethin'?"

"No, Miss Barbara — that's not how they taught
us to do it on 'Sesame Street'."

"It doesn't have to snow for Santa to get here.
His sleigh rides on air!"

"That Christmas music makes my eyes so happy they cry."

"I'm not tellin' ANYBODY what I want 'cept
Santa Claus -- not even Mommy!"

"PJ was frowning in this one...Billy moved in this one, and here Dolly's making a face. Let's just BUY our cards this year."

"Grandma, did you used to play with Santa Claus when you were a little girl?"

"Every time you open a Christmas card are you S'POSED to say, 'Did we send them one?'"

"...and then you take this street, and then that
street, then this street, and..."

"You know those packages hidden in your closet,
Mommy? We didn't find them."

"...and we're also proud of our lovely Karen who is 19 and an honor student again in her sophomore year at Penn. Brad is now a very handsome 17-year-old, 6 feet tall and starring on Central's basketball team. Our summer vacation this year took us first to the beautiful..."

"Look! Joseph is saying the Pledge of Allegiance."

"I guess Santa must have a work shop in Japan, too, 'cause that's where it says this doll was made."

"It's Grandma! I'll go open the presents for h..
I mean, the DOOR for her!"

"We're finished playin' with the Christmas toys. What can we do now?"

"Don't worry, Daddy, I'll clean up all this mess with the sweeper Santa brought me."

"I just wanted to know if it's New Year's yet so
I could put up my calendar."

"THE BOWL GAMES ARE STARTING!"

"Are you SURE Grandma said to put the money she gave us in the bank?"

"Can I wear this shirt again? The dirt's in the
back so it won't show."

"Know what Grandma has on her window sill?
A POT OF URANIUM!"

"Know how much I have? I have six moneys!"

"Look! There's a hijacker!"

"I have to get right back outside so all the kids can enjoy me."

"What time is it when the big hand is on zero
and the little hand is on fourteen?"

"Open the door and let
me in!"

"Not by the hair of my
chinny-chin-chin!"

"We're just bringin' some snow in to play with."

"I'm drawing a cat instead 'cause I can't spell 'giraffe'."

"I not here ---I with Daddy!"

"Bruce Durack is asking his mother if he can stay here for dinner."

"Mmm! Mommy! I wish you could get a job in there!"

"I sure hope Billy's guardian angel doesn't go on strike."

"How do you like the new glasses Mommy went
out and bought this afternoon?"

"When I die, can I take my blanket with me?"

"That's MY gum you found, Jeffy! And you know the old saying: 'Finders weepers, losers keepers'!"

"Can Lee Bell come over? I don't have anybody to play with."

"You're sitting there looking very cute and
I want you to stop it!"

"Isn't Barfy GOOD, Mommy? He's gettin' rid of
all the leftovers for us."

"Remember, Mommy, you only talk to the
teachers about me on PTA nights —
tonight's Open House!"

"Wait! Before you put the goldfish in, I have to
see if this water is the right temp'ture."

"Is it time to feed the goldfish yet?"

"Can I have some of the scraps for the goldfish?"

"There are TEN of us living in this house now --
me, Mommy, Dolly, Jeffy, PJ, Barfy, Sam,
Kittycat, the goldfish...let's see -- that's
nine...Kittycat, the goldfish, and...
oh, yeah -- Daddy!"

"If we don't clean the bowl very often, the water will get diluted."

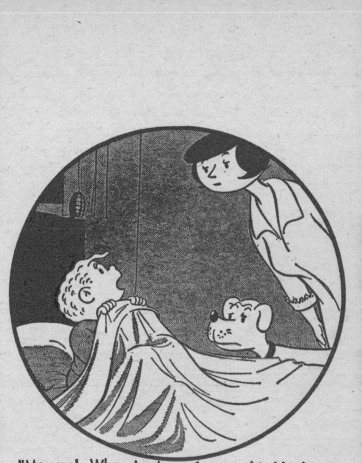

"Mommy! When I rub my feet on this blanket,
there are SPARKS under here!"

"Are most snowmen bald?"

"Instead of just writing 'Billy' on my lunch could
you put 'Wild Bill'?"

"Daddy, what's the date of the Fourth of July this year?"

"I smell something PURPLE!"

"I think we're havin' company. Mommy bought
'tato chips and pretzels and soda and..."

"Know what, Daddy? If you were a bird, you'd
be prettier than Mommy."

"I hope I get Miss Lee for a teacher next year
'cause I already know how to spell
her name."

"Did you know pennies can write?"

"I fell down, but I'm not sure if I hurt myself yet."

"PJ is two rulers high already!"

"Here comes Peter Cottontail...Hoppin' down
the money trail..."

"Mommy's telling us a Bible story 'bout a
PUNCHY PILOT."

"I got these pants for Easter and nobody EVER
wore them before!"

"I got a hit but somebody caught it before it hit the ground."

"Birds don't sing, they whistle. Right, Mommy?"

"How come you haven't been playing much with the presents we bought you for Mother's Day?"

"I'm going to put this hair of mine away and save it for 'Show and Tell' in college."

"What are these lollipops for, Grandma?"

"Who put the ice cream on the cereal shelf?"

"Mommy, this rose bush BIT me!"

"No, you CAN'T have a penny, PJ! Do you think money grows on weeds?"

"The can says this lemonade mix makes ONE quart, but we got FOUR quarts out of it!"

"Look! There's a hole in the sky and I can see a little bit of heaven!"

Have Fun with the Family Circus

ANY CHILDREN?	14116	$1.50
DADDY'S LITTLE HELPERS	14384	$1.50
DOLLY HIT ME BACK!	14273	$1.50
GOOD MORNING SUNSHINE!	14356	$1.50
FOR THIS I WENT TO COLLEGE?	14069	$1.50
NOT ME!	14333	$1.50
I'M TAKING A NAP	14144	$1.50
LOOK WHO'S HERE	14207	$1.50
PEACE, MOMMY, PEACE	14145	$1.50
PEEKABOO! I LOVE YOU!	14174	$1.50
WANNA BE SMILED AT?	14118	$1.50
WHEN'S LATER, DADDY?	14124	$1.50
MINE	14056	$1.50
SMILE!	14172	$1.50
JEFFY'S LOOKIN' AT ME!	14096	$1.50
CAN I HAVE A COOKIE?	14155	$1.50
THE FAMILY CIRCUS	14068	$1.50
HELLO, GRANDMA?	14169	$1.50
I NEED A HUG	14147	$1.50
QUIET! MOMMY'S ASLEEP!	13930	$1.50

Buy them at your local bookstore or use this handy coupon for ordering.

COLUMBIA BOOK SERVICE
32275 Mally Road, P.O. Box FB, Madison Heights, MI 48071

Please send me the books I have checked above. Orders for less than 5 books must include 75¢ for the first book and 25¢ for each additional book to cover postage and handling. Orders for 5 books or more postage is FREE. Send check or money order only.

Cost $_____   Name _____

Sales tax*_____   Address _____

Postage_____   City _____

Total $_____   State _____ Zip _____

* The government requires us to collect sales tax in all states except AK, DE, MT, NH and OR.

This offer expires 1 March 82